Explore and Protect
the Natural Wonders of the Sea

THE WORLD OF
CORAL REEFS

Erin Spencer

Illustrated by Alexandria Neonakis

Storey Publishing

Contents

Rainforests of the Sea, 4

A World of Coral, 6

The Great Barrier Reef, 8

Coral Close-Up, 10

The Building Blocks of Reefs, 12

Soft, Swaying Corals, 14

Coral Babies, 16

One Polyp Becomes Many, 18

A Reef Is Born, 20

A Hawaiian Creation Story, 22

An Ecosystem in Balance, 24

No Backbone? No Problem!, 26

So Many Fish!, 28

Large and in Charge, 30

Coral Reefs Help People, 32

Everything Is Connected, 34

The Reefs Need Our Help, 36

Trash Talk, 38

Warmer Oceans Hurt Corals, 40

Science at Work, 42

Glossary, 44

Going Deeper, 45

Index, 47

Rainforests of the Sea

Splash! Imagine you're swimming in a warm ocean. Bright blue water stretches as far as you can see. With your mask and snorkel, you peek below the surface. Before your eyes is an incredible underwater world!

You've just discovered one of the most unusual and important **ecosystems** in the ocean—a **coral reef**.

Corals may look like colorful rocks, but they're actually living animals.

Coral reefs are only a small part of the ocean, but they are home to millions of animals, including sharks, sea turtles, and octopuses. In fact, they have more plants and animals than almost any other place on Earth. Like rainforests, they are very important *habitats*. Some creatures who live there are found no place else.

How many animals can you spot around the reef?

A World of Coral

Coral reefs are found all over the world—including in some places you might not expect! Most reefs are in the warm, clear waters of the *tropics*. That's because many corals need warmth and lots of bright sunlight to grow.

 Warm-water coral reefs

Cold-water (deep-sea) coral reefs

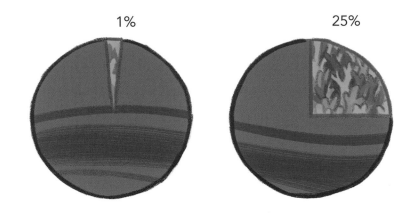

1%   25%

Coral reefs cover less than 1% of the ocean floor, but 25% of all ocean life depends on them!

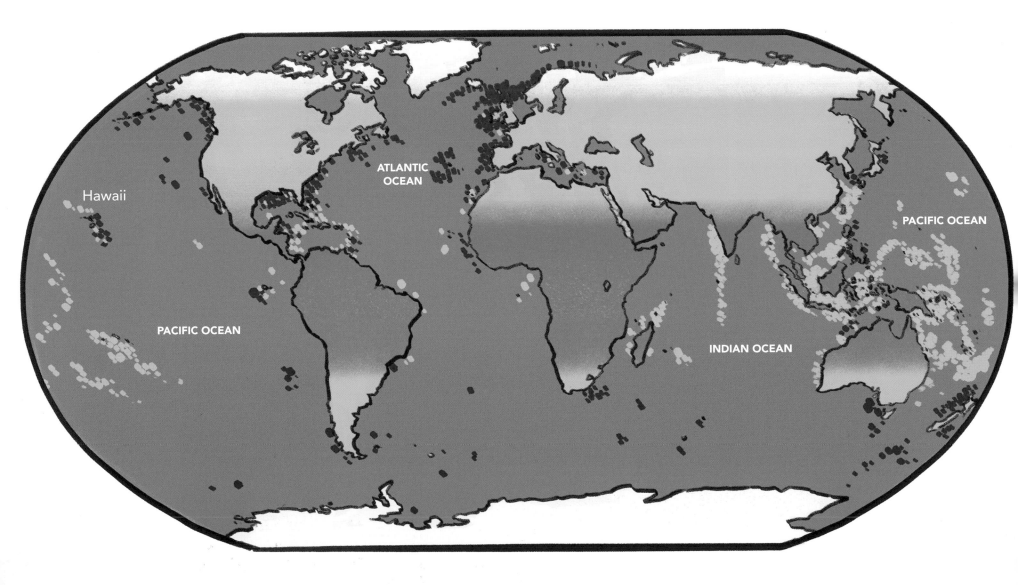

Hawaii

ATLANTIC OCEAN

PACIFIC OCEAN

PACIFIC OCEAN

INDIAN OCEAN

Most reef-building corals live in this shallow, sunny zone.

Not all corals need sunlight to live, though. Deep-sea corals can grow 20,000 feet (6,100 m) below the ocean surface, where sunlight doesn't reach.

The deep sea is pitch dark and cold, with temperatures close to freezing. That is *very* chilly compared to the warm tropical waters where shallow corals live!

Deep-sea corals are at home here in the cold and dark but don't live in the deepest ocean trenches.

Deep-sea soft corals

A black coral found near Hawaii is one of the oldest animals ever discovered. It is over 4,200 years old—almost as old as the pyramids of ancient Egypt!

The Great Barrier Reef

The Great Barrier Reef in Australia is the largest living structure in the world. It is made up of over 900 islands and almost 3,000 smaller reefs. All together it is over 1,429 miles (2,300 km) long. That's longer than 25,000 football fields!

The Great Barrier Reef is famous for its *biodiversity* because so many different animals and plants live there. It has over 400 types of coral and 1,500 types of fish.

Dugongs look like manatees and are related to elephants! They like to munch on the seagrass beds around the reef.

AUSTRALIA

Great
Barrier
Reef

The Great Barrier Reef
is so big, it can be seen
from space!

Clown fish have a special
relationship with stinging sea
anemones. The anemone's sting
doesn't hurt the clown fish. The
clown fish uses its bright colors
to lure in other fish for anemones
to eat, and anemones protect the
clownfish from getting eaten by
bigger fish.

Sea snakes look like snakes you
see on land, but they can swim.
They have sharp, *venomous* fangs.

9

Coral Close-Up

Time to take a closer look! See those little things that look like upside-down jellyfish? Those are called coral *polyps*. Polyps are the living animals that make up all the coral reefs around the world.

Coral polyps are clear. So why are corals so colorful? Polyps get their color from algae called *zooxanthellae* (*zoh-uh-zan-thell-ee*) that live in their bodies. The corals shelter the zooxanthellae, and the algae share food with the polyps. This is called a *mutualistic relationship*, meaning they help each other out!

Corals are related to jellyfish and anemones, which also have stinging tentacles.

10

A polyp stretches out its tentacles to look for food. These tentacles have stinging cells called *nematocysts*, which help polyps stun and capture tiny plankton to eat.

Zooxanthellae

Nematocysts are like miniature harpoons that shoot out of the tentacles!

Most coral polyps are smaller than your fingernail!

Tentacles

Mouth

Stomach

The Building Blocks of Reefs

There are thousands of species of coral! They all fall into two main types: *hard corals* and *soft corals*. Hard corals are also known as reef-building corals.

Polyps of hard corals create a tough outer skeleton made of *calcium carbonate* (also known as limestone). This outer skeleton protects the coral like a suit of armor protects a knight. If the polyp senses danger, it can pull its tentacles inside and keep them safe and sound.

MEET A FEW HARD CORALS

Hard corals grow in lots of shapes and sizes . . .

Staghorn corals have big branches that look like the antlers of a deer. When they grow together in a group, they make a dense tangle. This creates lots of nooks and crannies for critters to hide in.

Star corals are found in the Caribbean, around Florida, and in the Gulf of Mexico and can live for hundreds of years. They grow very slowly and can form mats or mounds of coral across a reef.

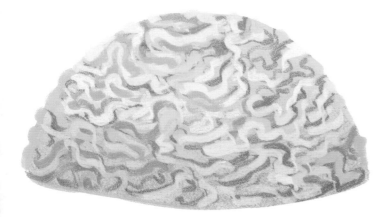

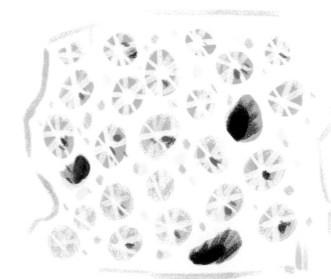

Skeleton of a hard coral

Brain corals look like a brain! They can grow over 6 feet (2 m) tall and live for 900 years.

Calcium helps make coral skeletons strong. It makes our human bones strong, too!

Soft, Swaying Corals

Soft corals are found on coral reefs, but they aren't reef-building like hard corals are. That's because they don't have tough outer skeletons. Many soft corals look like plants and can sway in the ocean currents. Both hard and soft corals are important parts of a healthy reef.

Soft corals still have tiny bits of calcium carbonate in their bodies. These spiky clumps are called sclerites and help the corals keep their shape.

MEET A FEW SOFT CORALS

There are many kinds of soft coral around the world . . .

Carnation corals are treelike, with tips that look like pillowy clouds. They are some of the most colorful soft corals and can be bright pink, purple, and orange.

Sea fans are a type of soft coral called a *gorgonian*. Although they don't have a calcium carbonate skeleton like hard corals, they do have a stiff structure inside that helps them keep their shape.

Leather corals have a tough leatherlike surface that inspired their name. They grow outward over the reef surface and form mats of coral.

Star polyps have beautiful bright tentacles with feathery branches called pinnules. They can be white, brown, or even green.

Coral Babies

Some species of coral reproduce by releasing eggs that turn into *planula*, or baby corals! These tiny corals are so small that you would need a microscope to see them.

Many hard corals release their eggs into the ocean in an event called spawning. The corals wait for the perfect time to release their eggs. Some will only spawn after a full moon!

Once the eggs become planula, they drift along in the ocean currents until they find a place to settle down.

Baby corals look for a hard place, like a rock, to land on. Once they find the perfect home, they attach to the surface and get ready to grow.

planula

FROM OLD TO NEW

New corals can also be made by *fragmentation*.

In this process, a small piece of coral breaks off of a larger one when disturbed by waves, storms, or other animals.

Then, over time, that small piece of coral grows larger and larger.

One Polyp Becomes Many

How do tiny reef-building coral polyps become big, beautiful reefs? After a polyp attaches to a hard surface like rock or other coral, it makes copies of itself, called buds. Many buds come together to form a **coral colony**.

The polyp builds its calcium carbonate armor around itself.

Over time, the polyp adds another layer beneath the first. Then another. Slowly, slowly, the polyp moves upward.

Sometimes, the polyp will split in two in a process called *budding*. This allows the coral colony to grow outward as well as up.

Most corals grow less than 1 inch (2.5 cm) per year, and can live for hundreds of years. Imagine building a house by putting one brick down every year. It would take a long time, but eventually you would have a house!

A Reef Is Born

When many coral colonies come together, they form a coral reef! There are a few different types of coral reefs.

lagoon

reef

reef

A fringing reef grows close to shore. It's the most common type of reef.

A barrier reef is separated from shore by a large lagoon of water. Can you guess the most famous barrier reef? (Hint: See page 8!)

An atoll grows in a circle and has a lagoon in the middle. From above, you can see a beautiful blue halo of water.

FROM ISLAND TO ATOLL

Over time, a reef can change from one type to another. Imagine an island in the middle of the ocean.

1. First, a fringing reef forms around the island.

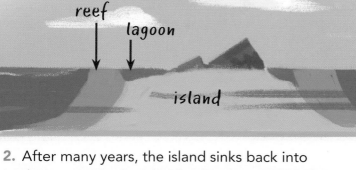

2. After many years, the island sinks back into the ocean. As the island sinks, the coral reef continues to grow. Eventually, a barrier reef forms.

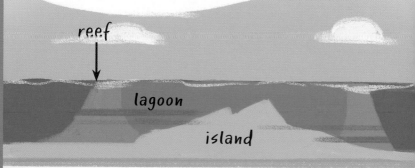

3. Over time, the island sinks completely beneath the ocean! You can still see the ring of coral from the surface, though. Now it is an atoll.

A Hawaiian Creation Story

The Hawaiian Islands lie in the middle of the Pacific Ocean, surrounded by fringing reefs, barrier reefs, and atolls.

Hina'ōpūhalako'a is the goddess of corals and spiny sea creatures. Legend has it that a chief named Māui got a special shell from Hina'ōpūhalako'a's reef.

From the reef, Hawaiians collect fish and shellfish to eat and supplies to make medicine. In turn, Native Hawaiians honor the reefs through religious ceremonies and storytelling.

Māui made the shell into a fishhook, which he used to pull together all the islands of Hawaii.

The Hawaiian creation story says that all life began with coral. In a sacred chant called the *Kumulipo*, the coral polyp was the very first animal born on Earth.

An Ecosystem in Balance

Native peoples like the Hawaiians have long understood that they are part of the amazing ecosystem that is the coral reef, where everything depends on everything else. Remember: 25 percent of all ocean life lives on a reef. So what makes the coral reef such a good home?

Coral reefs provide food and shelter for all kinds of animals . . .

Small fish hide in the nooks and crannies between coral colonies.

Sea cucumbers inch along the sand.

Worms burrow into the ocean floor.

Sunlight shines into shallow reefs to give plants and algae (including the corals' zooxanthellae!) the energy they need to grow. The plants and algae are eaten by animals on the reef, and those animals are eaten by even bigger ones.

Grouper, sharks, and other big fish swim over the reef, looking for food.

Turtles nibble on nearby seagrass.

No Backbone?
No Problem!

On a coral reef you will see two types of animals:
vertebrates, animals with backbones, and *invertebrates*,
animals without backbones. Many of the ocean's most
famous animals, including whales, fish, and sea turtles, have
backbones, just like humans do. But most of the animals
in the world (97 percent) are invertebrates, including coral
polyps! Here are just a few.

Nudibranchs are sea
slugs. Many are toxic.
Their bright colors warn
predators to stay away.

Feather stars look like billowing
plants, but they're actually
related to starfish. They can
use their feathery arms to swim
through the water.

Octopuses are some of the smartest animals in the sea. They can change their color and shape to blend into their surroundings. Their *camouflage* helps them hide from predators and sneak up on prey!

Sponges are *sessile* animals, meaning they stay in one place (just like coral). They move water through their bodies and filter out tiny pieces of food to eat.

Snapping shrimp are small, but they pack a big punch. When they snap shut their big claw, it makes a jet of water and bubbles so powerful that it can stun or kill small animals that the shrimp eats. Snapping shrimps are some of the loudest animals in the ocean!

So Many Fish!

Thousands of species of fish make their homes on coral reefs. Some are *herbivores*, meaning they eat plants. Other fish are *carnivores*, meaning they eat other animals.

Fish on the reef come in all shapes, sizes, and colors! Which one is your favorite?

Scorpion fish have camouflage that helps them blend into the reef, where they wait to attack small fish that swim by. *Snap!*

Goatfish have long whiskers they push into the sand to find worms and other small invertebrates.

Frogfish have special fins that look like legs. They use them to walk along the ocean floor! They also have a dangling lure that acts as a fishing rod to attract small fish and shrimp to eat. Tricky!

Mandarinfish have neon blue, orange, and yellow stripes that make them look like they were colored with bright markers.

Lionfish have bold stripes and a mane of venomous spines down their back.

Parrotfish munch on algae that grow on coral. This helps keep the coral clean and healthy.

Large and in Charge

Coral reefs are home to BIG animals, too! Rays glide gracefully through the water while massive sharks cruise around looking for their next meal. Sharks are an important part of a healthy reef. They are top predators who feed on fish, octopuses, turtles, and more.

Blacktip reef sharks get their name from the black tips of their fins. They can grow up to 6 feet (2 m) long and like to hang out in the shallow waters of the reef.

Reef manta rays are some of the most graceful animals on the reef. Their "wingspan" can reach over 11 feet (3.4 m)! They are filter feeders, meaning they eat tiny plankton that they sift out of the water.

Spotted moray eels can be hard to find. They like to hide in cracks and crevices in the reef. They can't see very well, so they rely on their sharp sense of smell to find their meals.

Hawksbill sea turtles are known for their beautifully patterned shells. They can be found swimming on coral reefs all over the world, searching for their favorite food—sponges!

Coral Reefs Help People

Ocean animals aren't the only ones who rely on coral reefs. People need them, too. It doesn't matter whether you live near a reef or far away—reefs help all of us.

Reefs give us food. Do you like to eat fish? People all over the world eat fish that are caught near reefs.

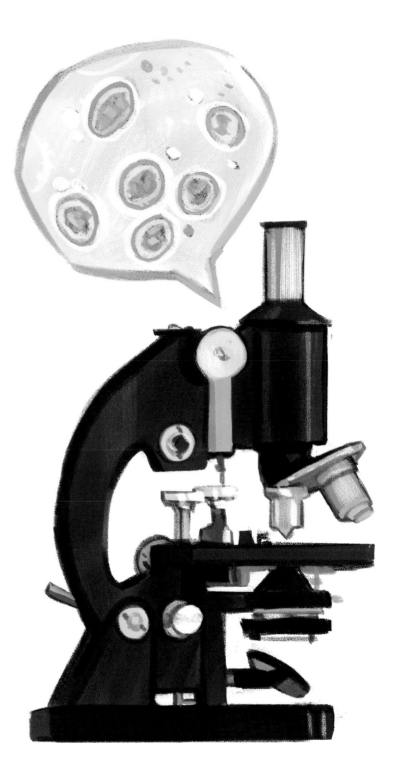

Reefs help us find new medicines. By studying animals and plants on coral reefs, scientists have found new ways to treat cancer and other diseases.

Reefs protect us from storms. They keep buildings and homes along the shore safer by making big waves less powerful.

Reefs are fun! People travel from far away to swim, snorkel, dive, and fish along coral reefs. It's important to make sure we can enjoy reefs in ways that don't hurt the coral or other animals who live there.

Everything Is Connected

We are all part of the same beautiful planet, Earth. Most of Earth is covered in ocean, so a healthy planet depends on a healthy ocean. And a healthy ocean depends on healthy reefs.

When coral reefs are sick, we all need to work together to help them get better. When the reefs thrive, we all thrive.

E mālama i ke kai, na ke kai e mālama iā 'oe. "Take care of the ocean, it is the ocean that will take care of you."
—HAWAIIAN SAYING

The Reefs Need Our Help

Life on the reef is getting harder. One challenge is keeping the water clean, especially as more people live and work near the ocean.

Corals need clean water to live. Big factories, construction work, and large farms often send dirty water into the ocean. But there are ways YOU can cut down on *pollution* right from your own home.

Small rivers flow into big rivers, which flow into the ocean far away—which means that no matter where you live, you can make a difference.

Use ocean-friendly products in your yard and garden. Ask your parents to choose non-toxic chemicals when they can, and avoid using lots of fertilizer. It's better for people, too!

Use less water. Cutting back on water use means less dirty water getting back to the sea. Try taking a shorter shower and turning off the faucet while you brush your teeth.

Trash Talk

You wouldn't want to swim around in trash, would you? Neither do ocean animals! Some of the trash we create on land ends up in the ocean, and it can hurt coral reefs and the animals who live there.

Animals can become entangled in trash like old fishing nets, making it hard for them to swim.

Fish and turtles can also accidently eat garbage that looks like food. To a sea turtle, a plastic bag can look like a yummy jellyfish.

But there's good news: We can all help keep trash out of the ocean! Try to make less trash in the first place, reuse things when you can, and recycle plastic bottles and aluminum cans.

You can also clean up trash at beaches, rivers, or the ocean near you! Just make sure to ask an adult for help if you see anything sharp or heavy.

TIPS FOR LESS TRASH

▸ Use a reusable bag when shopping.

▸ Skip plastic water bottles, and fill up a reusable bottle.

▸ Pack a reusable fork and spoon with your lunch.

▸ Ditch plastic straws for metal or paper ones.

▸ Use cloth dish towels instead of paper towels.

Warmer Oceans Hurt Corals

Climate change is when the earth's average conditions, like temperature, change over time. Because of climate change, the ocean is getting warmer. When corals get hot and stressed, they kick out the colorful zooxanthellae living in their bodies. This is called *coral bleaching*.

Healthy corals are bright and full of life.

Bleached corals are totally white. Warmer temperatures can also cause corals to get sick more easily.

Climate change is caused by gases in the earth's atmosphere. A lot of these gases come from burning fuels in cars and factories, raising animals for food, and using electricity. Many people are working to cut down on these gases, and you can help.

Turn off lights when you're not in the room. Replace old lightbulbs with energy-efficient ones.

Unplug things when you're not using them.

Bike or walk instead of driving, if you can. When you do drive, try to carpool.

Eat less meat, maybe by encouraging your family to pick one "meatless" day a week.

Support climate organizations by volunteering or raising money.

Write a letter to your local politicians to tell them why climate action is important to you.

Science at Work

People all around the world are working to help coral reefs. There is still a lot we don't know about them! Scientists are studying reefs in the lab and in the ocean. They are trying to figure out what will happen to corals in the future—especially as the ocean gets warmer.

Scientists and volunteers use scuba gear to breathe underwater and get close to the reef.

Some scientists are "planting" small coral pieces on reefs to help them grow into new colonies.

Some coral reefs are protected, meaning there are rules about what you can and can't do near the reef. These areas help keep the reef ecosystems safe.

Smile! Underwater cameras can help scientists see which animals use the reef all day and night.

Close your eyes and picture all the wonderful animals of the reef— tiny coral polyps, colorful parrotfish, stunning reef sharks, and more. They all depend on us to protect their priceless coral reef habitat.

We can do it, together!

43

Glossary

atoll. A reef that forms a ring with a lagoon in the middle

barrier reef. A reef that is separated from land by a lagoon of water

biodiversity. The number of different living organisms in a place

budding. When a coral polyp clones itself and creates a new polyp

calcium carbonate. A substance made of calcium, oxygen, and carbon that makes up the skeleton of hard corals

camouflage. When an organism's color or shape helps it blend into its surroundings

carnivore. An animal that eats other animals

climate change. A significant change in Earth's average conditions over time

coral bleaching. When stress causes coral polyps to kick out the zooxanthellae that live inside them, turning the corals white

coral colony. A group of identical coral polyps living together

coral reef. An underwater structure made up of the skeletons of many coral colonies

ecosystem. All living organisms and nonliving physical features of an area

fragmentation. When coral breaks off a parent colony and forms a new colony

fringing reef. A coral reef that grows close to the shore

gorgonian. A type of soft coral

habitat. The area where an animal, plant, or other organism lives

hard coral. A type of coral with a hard external skeleton, also known as "reef-building coral"

herbivore. An animal that eats plants

Hinaʻōpūhalakoʻa. Hawaiian goddess of corals and spiny sea creatures

invertebrate. An animal without a backbone

Kumulipo. A sacred Hawaiian chant that describes the creation of life on Earth

Māui. An ancient chief in Hawaiian and other Polynesian myths

mutualistic relationship. When two organisms work together and both benefit, like coral and zooxanthellae

nematocyst. A stinging cell in corals and some other organisms that looks like a small harpoon

planula. A free-swimming baby coral

pollution. Harmful materials that enter the environment

polyp. The living organism that makes up coral colonies

predator. An animal that lives by hunting other animals

sclerites. Small clumps of calcium carbonate found in soft corals

sessile. An organism that stays in one place

soft coral. A type of coral that does not produce a hard external skeleton

spawning. When corals release their eggs into the water to reproduce

tropics. Locations that are close to the earth's equator; most reefs are found here

venomous. When an organism can insert toxins by biting or stinging

vertebrate. An animal with a backbone

zooxanthellae. Small algae that live in coral polyps and give coral its color

Going Deeper

Want to learn more about coral reefs? The following resources offer much more to discover about topics covered in this book.

Reefs around the World

You don't need a snorkel or a plane ticket to discover coral reefs. Thanks to underwater 3D imaging technology, you can take a virtual dive from your own computer! To explore interactive photos and videos, take a look at these websites:

Google Earth
https://earth.app.goo.gl/xe8nDQ
- Dive into 3D underwater scenes
- Choose from over a dozen reefs around the world
- Read facts about reef locations

XL Catlin Seaview Survey
https://catlinseaviewsurvey.com
- Take interactive virtual dives
- Explore 12 reefs around the world
- Observe a coral bleaching event

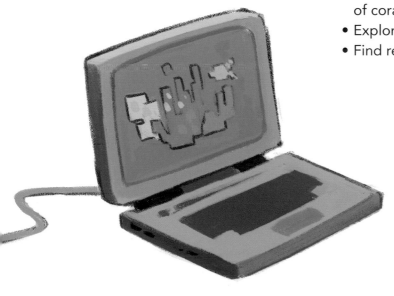

Biology of Coral

Corals have evolved incredible strategies to grow and thrive on the reef. Videos, photos, and 3D models allow us to see these processes for ourselves, helping us to understand how corals have survived in the ocean for so long. To explore in-depth illustrations and videos of coral polyps, see:

Khaled bin Sultan Living Oceans Foundation
https://livingoceansfoundation.org/education/e-learning
- Discover 12 units covering coral feeding, life cycle, and more
- Try quizzes, art projects, interactive videos, and at-home labs

PBS Learning Media: Marine Science
https://pbslearningmedia.org/collection/marine-science
- See interactive models and videos of coral
- Explore microscopic processes
- Find resources for kids of all ages

Threats Facing Reefs

Coral reefs are facing a range of threats, from climate change and plastic pollution to overfishing and habitat loss. To learn about ocean threats and discover ways to take action, see:

Environmental Protection Agency: The Planet Protectors
https://epa.gov/students/planet-protectors-activities-kids
- Accept the mission to reduce waste as a Planet Protector
- Solve puzzles and games around trash and recycling

NASA Climate Kids
https://climatekids.nasa.gov
- Read kid-friendly facts on climate change
- Play games around coral bleaching
- Explore "big questions" about climate

Ocean Conservancy: Clean Swell
https://oceanconservancy.org/trash-free-seas/international-coastal-cleanup/cleanswell
- Download the Clean Swell app to track the trash you collect
- Earn badges and learn ocean pollution facts

Coral Conservation

People around the world are working hard to protect coral reef ecosystems. To learn about conservation programs and even participate, see:

Fragments of Hope
https://fragmentsofhope.org
- Learn about coral planting programs in Belize
- Visit the Teacher's Corner for more resources

NASA NeMO-Net
www.nemonet.info
- Play a 3D coral identification video game
- Become a citizen scientist and contribute to a NASA database

Reef Biodiversity

Coral reefs are home to countless plants and animals of all shapes and sizes—and we're discovering new species all the time. To explore more animals who live on the reef, see:

The Ocean Image Bank
https://www.theoceanagency.org/ocean-image-bank
- Dive into dozens of photo galleries
- Download and share professional photos
- Sort photos by location or animal type

Monterey Bay Aquarium Animal Cams
https://montereybayaquarium.org/animals/live-cams
- Enjoy live video feeds from many exhibits, including coral reefs and sharks
- Read animal and habitat facts, download wallpapers, and more

National Geographic Animal Facts
https://nationalgeographic.com/animals/facts-pictures
- Search a huge database for ocean animal facts
- Explore galleries of fish, invertebrates, mammals, and more

CURRICULUM GUIDES FOR EDUCATORS

We cover a wide range of topics in this book, including coral biology, evolution, coral reef food webs, threats facing reefs, and current research—and there is still more to explore! Check out our downloadable curriculum guide to learn how you can include the content in this book in your classroom. The guide includes suggested articles, videos, and activities that dive further into coral reef ecosystems, climate change, pollution, and trash. Activities target a range of age groups and can be completed on the computer or with materials found around the house.

Visit https://www.storey.com/the-world-of-coral-reefs-educators-guide.

Index

A

algae, 10, 25, 29
anemones, 9, 10
atolls, 21, 22
Australia, Great Barrier Reef in, 8–9

B

barrier reefs, 20, 22. *See also* Great
    Barrier Reef
biodiversity, 8
bleaching, coral, 40
buds/budding, 18–19

C

calcium/calcium carbonate, 12, 13, 14, 20
camouflage, 27, 28
carnivores and herbivores, 28
climate change, 40–41
clown fish, 9
cold water corals/coral reefs, 6, 7
coral bleaching, 40
coral colony, 18–19
corals, types of, 7, 13, 15. *See also*
    specific type
creation story, Hawaiian, 22–23

D

deep-sea corals/coral reefs, 6, 7
dugongs, 8

E

ecosystems, 4, 24–25, 34–35, 43
eels, spotted moray, 31
environment, protecting our, 36–39, 41

F

feather stars, 26
fish, 24, 25, 28–29, 38. *See also specific type*
food, coral reefs providing, 32
fragmentation of coral, 17
fringing reefs, 20, 21, 22
frogfish, 28

G

goatfish, 28
goddess of corals, Hawaiian, 22
Great Barrier Reef, 8–9
grouper, 25

H

habitats, 5, 43
hard corals, 12, 13, 16
Hawaii/Hawaiians, 7, 22–23, 24, 34
herbivores and carnivores, 28

I

invertebrates, 26–27
islands, 21. *See also* Hawaii/Hawaiians

L

lagoons, 21
lionfish, 29

M

mandarinfish, 29
manta rays, reef, 30
medicines, coral reefs and, 22, 32
mutualistic relationship, 10

N

nematocysts, 11
nudibranchs, 26

O

oceans, 4–7, 24, 40–41
octopuses, 5, 27

P

parrotfish, 29, 43
people, reefs helping, 32–33
plankton, 11, 30
plants, 8, 25
planula, 16–17

polyps, coral, 10, 11, 12, 15, 19, 20, 23, 43
predators, 26, 27, 30

R

Reef, Great Barrier, 8–9
reef formation, 12–13, 20–21

S

science at work, reef study and, 42–43
sclerites, 14
scorpion fish, 28
sea cucumbers, 24
sea fans, 15
sea snakes, 9
sessile animals, 27
sharks, 5, 25, 30, 43
shrimp, snapping, 27
soft, swaying corals, 7, 12, 14–15
spawning, hard corals and, 16
sponges, 27, 31
staghorn and star corals, 13
star polyps, 15
storms, reefs protecting us from, 33

T

tentacles, 10, 11, 12, 15
trash, pollution and, 36, 38–39
tropics, 6
turtles, 5, 25, 26, 30, 31, 38

V

vertebrates, 26

W

warmer oceans, climate change and, 40–41
warm water corals/coral reefs, 6, 7
water, using less, 37
worms, 24

Z

zooxanthellae, 10, 11, 25, 40

Dedicated to my parents,
who taught me to love books
and the sea. This is for you.

Thank you to the incredible
team at Storey Publishing,
especially Alethea Morrison
and Hannah Fries, for bringing
this book to life. I'm also
grateful to those who have
encouraged me to combine
my love of science and writing,
including Michelle Frey, Andrea
Leitch, and Dr. Ann Marie
Stock—I hope to support
others in the way you've
supported me.

Thank you to my family,
given and chosen, for their
unwavering support. And
a special thank you to my
husband, Corbin—facing each
day with you is the greatest
joy of my life.

The mission of Storey Publishing is to serve our customers by
publishing practical information that encourages
personal independence in harmony with the environment.

Edited by Alethea Morrison and Hannah Fries
Art direction and book design by Alethea Morrison
Text production by Liseann Karandisecky
Indexed by Christine R. Lindemer, Boston Road Communications
Illustrations by © Alexandria Neonakis

Text © 2022 by Erin T. Spencer

Storey books are available at special discounts when purchased in bulk for premiums
and sales promotions as well as for fund-raising or educational use. Special editions
or book excerpts can also be created to specification. For details, please call 800-
827-8673, or send an email to sales@storey.com.

Storey Publishing
210 MASS MoCA Way
North Adams, MA 01247
storey.com

Printed in China through Asia Pacific Offset
10 9 8 7 6 5 4 3 2 1

Library of Congress Cataloging-in-Publication Data on file